I0171240

Prophecy, Transition & Miracles

Healing Nations

■ ■ ■

By Prince Handley

University of Excellence Press

Copyright © 2015 by Prince Handley
All Rights Reserved.

UNIVERSITY OF EXCELLENCE PRESS
Los Angeles ■ London ■ Tel Aviv

ISBN-13: 978-0692386019
ISBN-10: 0692386017

Printed in the U.S.A.

First Edition

The only Creative Prophecy book you need

TABLE OF CONTENTS

FOREWORD

One of the greatest areas of ministry that is still being overlooked—and under sought after—is **the office of Prophet.**

God uses prophets for different reasons and for different prophetic discourses. One of the greatest needs today for the office of Prophet is in **the capacity of "Spotter."**

Ethnic deliverance is in the "game plan" of the End Times of Planet Earth. **Prophetic creative decrees** will be one method by which God brings this about.

Also, **prophecy and specific healing words** will come to the forefront in the End Times resulting in MIRACLES sent by God for signs following these decrees.

The office of Prophet is feared by Satan. Many schemes are—and will be devised—by the enemy to divert, diffuse and dilute this office. This book—through revealed knowledge by the Spirit—provides the reader with **Intel to prevent this**.

The reader—and potential candidate for the office of Prophet—will study the **strategy of ethnic deliverance—healing nations—and MIRACLES**.

This book will show you HOW God works behind the scenes to help YOU become an **instrument of national deliverance**.

Prophecy, Transition & Miracles

Healing Nations

■ ■ ■

THE NEED FOR PROPHETS

You need to be continually in the **blessing zone**. In this book—among other important things—I will share with you two (2) important areas where members of the Body of Messiah—possibly including YOU—are being cheated out of blessing.

   ■ Not listening for the call to be a Prophet; and,

   ■ Not recognizing and honoring a Prophet.

Let's look at a few scriptures from both the Tanakh and the Brit Chadashah (New Testament) that are descriptive concerning the office—the calling—of a prophet.

> *"Now therefore restore the man his wife; for he is a **prophet**, and he shall pray for you, and you shall live: and if you restore her not, you can know that you shall surely die, you, and all that are yours."*
>
> — Genesis 20:7

> *"He that receives a **prophet** in the name of a prophet will receive a prophet's reward."*
>
> — Yeshua (Jesus) / Matthew 10:41

> *"He let no man do them wrong: Yes, he reproved leaders of nations for their sakes, saying, 'Touch not mine anointed, and do my **prophets** no harm.'"*
>
> — Psalm 105:15

In my book, *Conflict Healing,* I describe several incidents where people had opposed me in my ministry and what happened to them as a result:

> ▪ One lady drove her brand new yellow Cadillac through the back wall of her garage and into the swimming pool—could have drowned, but for

6

God's mercy—and was on the front page of three large newspapers:

Los Angeles Times

Long Beach Press Telegram

Orange County (previously Santa Ana) Register.

■ One young man died of a brain hemorrhage in 24 hours.

■ One lady's house was destroyed to the ground in 48 hours.

These are just a few, plus several I did NOT include in the book.

Remember when Elijah withstood and challenged the false prophets on Mt. Carmel, and called fire down from Heaven (1 Kings 18)? I was laughing the other day remembering when I was holding a tent meeting in Tennessee (USA). We had to cut down tall trees from the woods and drag them in by tractor to make poles to hold up the tent. One morning I was in the woods by myself praying for that night's meeting and asking God to **answer by fire from Heaven**.

I was kneeling in the woods on a tree stump and all of a sudden I heard noises. I looked around and on every side of me there were BIG black bulls. Immediately I thought of the scripture in Psalm 22:11-12, *"Be not far from me; for trouble is near; for there is none to help. Many bulls have compassed me: strong bulls of Bashan have beset me round.*" I don't know if I have ever prayed harder in my life! I prayed and prayed and prayed—and stayed and stayed and stayed—until finally the bulls moved away out of sight. Talk about being delivered!

Well, that night I preached on Elijah confronting the false prophets and calling down fire from Heaven. God had really been blessing the meetings and college students were driving from 70 miles away to come to the meetings. When I ended the meeting that night, I prayed, **"Hear me, O LORD God, and let fire come down from Heaven."** All of a sudden, smoke began to enter the tent from above!!! One of the large lights at the top of the wooden pole near the front where I was preaching overheated and **started burning the wooden pole** ... and **people ran to the altar**. One college student fell on the ground—under the power of the Holy Spirit—and remained there under the power of God. At that time in my life I was NOT baptized in the Holy Spirit and I did not know what was happening to the young man.

Several college students gave their lives to be missionaries for the LORD God that night. And one of the students was later raised up to be a pastor in that area. **It does NOT matter HOW God works ... just so He works.**

Elijah was a man—a human being—just like we are.

8

Yet, he prayed and God stopped the rain for three years. He prayed again, and God brought rain back on the earth again. **Elijah was NOT afraid to confront the leader of the nation.** Where are the REAL prophets today? **Sin is rampant because the office of the Prophet is being neglected: being vacated.**

One of the greatest areas of ministry that is still being overlooked—and under sought after—is the office of Prophet. Let me repeat: there are two (2) important areas where the enemy wants to cheat the Body of Messiah—to rob the synagogue and church—out of blessing. These attacks from the enemy are designed to deceive God's People so that they will:

> ▪ NOT listen to the call to be a Prophet; or,

> ▪ NOT recognize and honor the office of the Prophet.

Of course, NOT all of God's People are called to the office of Prophet. However, the sad thing is—due to bad, inaccurate teaching from teachers and seminaries—most people do NOT know there is such an office. I am NOT talking here about the Gift of Prophecy. I am talking about the **office** of the Prophet.

God uses prophets for different reasons and for different prophetic discourses. Prophecy can be:

9

■ Directed (to a particular person or group)

■ Specific (as to present or future action or resulting from past action)

■ National (pertaining to a country or ethnic amalgamation)

■ Judgmental (resulting from transgression of God's principles)

■ Contradictory (against false prophecies being declared)

■ Notification of blessing (due to God's favor or the result of obedience)

To the above mentioned I want to ADD a category that is often overlooked by rabbis, ministers and theologians: **Prophecy can be used by God through the Prophet as a "Spotter."** Let me give you an example. If you follow NASCAR racing you may be familiar with the term "Spotter." **A high speed professional auto racer definitely needs a Spotter**: a person who is also **an experienced driver but who is an observer of the race in a special location above** the crowd who can see the cars, the line up of drivers, the track condition and opportunities for the driver to go ahead and pass, as well as pitfalls for the driver to avoid. **Many times the ministry of the Prophet is used in similar—parallel—life circumstances: to direct and guide people or nations through troubled waters.**

The prophetic spotter will be much needed in the future with genome alteration, human enhancement, brain-machine interfacing and cyber—*artificial*—intelligence. *"Surely the Lord GOD will do nothing, but he reveals His secret unto his servants the prophets."* – Amos 3:7

You need to be continually in the blessing zone. One prerequisite for this is that **you need to be always listening to God ... and be open to what He is saying.** God does NOT change. And, the office of the Prophet has NOT changed. If you are NOT listening and someone calls you for dinner, you will probably miss dinner. **Are YOU listening to determine IF God is calling YOU to the office of Prophet?** And, I am NOT just talking to men. I am addressing this question to women—and girls—as well. **Women have been used since time past in the office of Prophet ... as well as men.**

Huldah was a Prophet. **Huldah is one of the seven women prophets of Israel enumerated by the Rabbis: Sarah, Miriam, Deborah, Hannah, Abigail, Huldah and Esther** (BT Megillah 14a). She is also mentioned among the twenty-three truly upright and righteous women who came forth from Israel (Midrash *Tadshe*, *Ozar ha-Midrashim* [Eisenstein], p. 474).

When King Josiah found the Torah scroll in the House of the Lord, he sent messengers to the prophet Huldah, **and not to Jeremiah**, probably hoping that she would exhibit feminine mercy in her prophecy (BT *Megillah* 14b). Josiah apparently hoped that Huldah would be more moderate in her revelations, or that she would "water down" the message of future troubles. However, contrary to his expectations, **Huldah delivered hard prophecies for the king.**

The greatest meetings where I have been on stage to observe closely as a minister were at the meetings of Kathryn Kulhman. Miss Kuhlman used to say often, *"If God would have found a man to do this job, he would NOT have chosen me."* I say that to emphasize—**and to prophesy**—that **God is getting ready to raise up and call out women as Prophets in these last days**: Holy women filled with the Ruach HaKodesh (the Holy Spirit), filled with His Word, and who operate in the Gifts of the Spirit—**women who are NOT afraid to confront the leaders of nations**, openly or otherwise!

As when God calls men, so it is when He calls women. Your background is NOT the reason for your calling. **Who you are** does NOT depend on what you have or do not have, what education you have or do not have, what you do or do not do, who you know or do not know, or what you have done or have not done.

God calls YOU because of WHAT you will do and WHO is in you.

Huldah answered the messengers from King Josiah when they came to hear the Word of the LORD from her: *"Tell the man who sent you to me."* (2 Kings 22:15) Ancient Rabbis comment that because of her haughty deportment, she was given a derogatory name, *"huldah,"* meaning "weasel" (BT *Megillah* 14b). However, I believe that Huldah may have possibly been—previously—a "sneaky, untrustworthy, or insincere person" until the God of Israel changed her and called her to be a Prophet. (Just like He changed Jacob, Moses and, just like He has changed—or, will change—many people reading this, including me.)

In Psalm 68:11, we read: *"The Lord gave the word: great was the company of those that published it."* The literal translation of *"**Great was the company of those that published it"** is: "**Of the female preachers there was a great host.**"* God has always used women. **God does NOT change—neither has the office of Prophet changed.**

*"And the next day we that were of Paul's company departed, and came unto Caesarea: and we entered into the house of Philip the evangelist, which was one of the seven; and abode with him. And the same man had **four daughters, virgins, which did prophesy**.*" – Acts 21:8-9

Several decades ago I prophesied that God was going to start raising up African Americans—and other Black People—for leadership in government, business and ministry and placing them in strategic positions. Now, I prophesy to you that God is going to raise up KEY women He has chosen for the office of Prophet.

The fringe benefits that go with the office of Prophet are wonderful. *"He let no man do them wrong: Yes, he reproved leaders of nations for their sakes, saying, 'Touch not mine anointed, and do my prophets no harm.'"* – Psalm 105:15

Now, let me give you a second prophecy. I want to quote from Ecclesiastes 3:1. *"To every thing there is a season, and a time to every purpose under the heaven."* My friend, **you are beginning to enter a NEW season. Your life is NOT over ... it is just beginning ... if you will receive this word and believe this prophecy**. You are entering a NEW season, my friend. Listen to God, obey God, be used by God ... and be BLESSED by God.

God has given you everything you need to **stay in the blessing zone.** Check to see if you are:

■ Listening to God's call to be a Prophet; and,

■ Recognizing and honoring the office of the Prophet.

And, if you need help making a decision—or if you feel that you have NOT recognized and honored the office of a particular Prophet—check out the following books titled, *Decision Making 101* ... AND ... *Conflict Healing – Relational Health.* **PLUS**, *How to Receive God's Power with Gifts of the Spirit,* which will enable you to receive God's Power with resultant gifts.

YOUR NEXT TRANSITION

After 40 years of wilderness wandering, the people of Israel - the believers under Joshua - were ready to pass over the Jordan into the Promised Land. They had NOT passed that way before. Therefore, they let the Ark of the Covenant lead them about 2,000 cubits, as they were commanded by Joshua. [Joshua 3:4] **By following the presence of the LORD they would know which way to go.**

You are NOT to jump ahead of the LORD but to honor His holiness, just as the people honored the sacredness of the Ark. **Let God lead you . . . and then follow Him in faith**. Then you can pass over and make the transition to the Promised Land: the completion of the Holy Spirit goals you have prayed for so long! He understands when you're not sure; but He also understands when you don't obey.

Notice that after they crossed over, the people of Israel came up from the Jordan on the tenth day of the first month, and they camped in Gilgal on the east border of

Jericho. God chose that day—**just as He chooses the days of your deliverance and transition**—if you follow Him and honor His holiness! Every detail, including the exact nanosecond of your MIRACLES, are known by God, prepared by God, and depend upon your obedience in following His commands in faith!

IF you are a believer and follower of Messiah Yeshua, every deliverance, every healing, **every transition in your life**—even your employment or unemployment—**is rooted in the Passover**: the shed BLOOD of the Lamb of God. **Plead the BLOOD—rely on THE BLOOD—when the Spirit is leading you in NEW transitions**. Your victory is contained in and assured by THE BLOOD!

That first day in the Promised Land (Joshua 4:19)—after passing over the Jordan River—was the fulfillment of God's promise and also the day when the lamb was selected: the tenth day of the first month [March-April, the month of Nisan, also called Abib - see Exodus Chapter 12]. The Passover would be four days later.

"Now the children of Israel camped in Gilgal, and kept the Passover on the fourteenth day of the month at twilight on the plains of Jericho." [Joshua 5:10] They ate the produce of the land on the next day, unleavened bread and parched grain. The next day the manna ceased.

Notice: God always provides the NEW provision of the NEW transition before He cuts off the OLD provision.

He is a good Father! Don't worry—just follow His holy presence as he leads you.

Sometimes we are so concerned with the minors that we're missing the majors! Forget the details and follow God. **He Who leads you into the NEW transition will also lead you into the intricacies of the details**. Just MOVE, implement, and take care of the refinements later. Obey God!

Like the monkey holding on to the banana in the jar who couldn't get his hand out to enjoy the banana, so many people are "holding on" to their ministries or professions that they cannot be released for NEW transition into greater service and works for the glory of the LORD, and for their blessing as well.

God knows exactly where you are at this time in your journey with Him. And so do you! **Do you want to go on to conquer and attain those Holy Spirit goals you have prayed and fasted for so long?** Then listen carefully to Him. Are you willing to make the transition from your comfort zone to a blessed place where millions—possibly billions—of people will be blessed by your life service or ministry?

VICTORY IN YOUR TRANSITION

The simple things are usually the powerful things. And so it is in the plan of God which He gives you for victory. **Be willing and obey** is the admonition of the prophet Isaiah:

"If you are willing and obedient you will eat the good of the land; but if you refuse and rebel, you will be devoured with the sword: for the mouth of the LORD has spoken it." (Isaiah 1:19-20)

The beautiful purpose of this—and **the LOVE of God—is shown in the previous verse**:

"Come now, and let us reason together, says the LORD: though your sins are as scarlet, they will be white as snow; though they are red like crimson, they will be as wool." (Verse 18)

Israel's **unbelief** (except for Caleb and Joshua) that they could take the Promised Land resulted in 40 years of wilderness wandering. **Have you been wandering long?**

Do you have great Spirit given goals that have been in you heart and prayers for years but have not come to fruition yet? Is it because you have failed to GO into the Promised Land—to make that transition in FAITH? Have you been waiting for everything to fall into place before you leave your comfort zone?

Let Me repeat: Like the monkey holding on to the banana in the jar, that couldn't get his hand out to enjoy the banana, **are you "holding on"** to your ministry …

18

your business ... your toys—**not releasing them—so that you can make a NEW transition into greater service and works** for the glory of God, and for your blessing as well?

☑ UNBELIEF WILL BLOCK YOUR TRANSITION!

When the children of Israel were about to attack Jericho, Joshua—with the direction of the LORD—commanded the people, *"You shall NOT shout or make any noise with your voice, nor shall a word proceed out of your mouth, until the day I say unto you, 'Shout!' Then you shall shout."* (Joshua 6:10) They were commanded to keep silence for seven days.

☑ AT THE ONSET OF GREAT WORKS FOR GOD, DON'T TALK MUCH AND—ABOVE ALL—DO NOT SPEAK WORDS OF FEAR AND UNBELIEF!

The spoils of Jericho were like the first fruits of harvest. It was the first city they conquered in the Promised Land: their first stage of the victory promised. And God commanded them NOT to keep the spoils of the city for themselves.

"And you, in any wise keep yourselves from the accursed thing, lest you make yourselves accursed, when you take of the accursed thing, and make the camp of Israel a curse, and trouble it. But all the silver, and gold, and vessels of brass and iron, are

19

consecrated unto the LORD: they shall come into the treasury of the LORD." (Joshua 6:18-19)

The Hebrew root for the word "**accursed**" is "**cherem**" and it ALSO means the "**devoted thing**" or a "**dedicated thing**" depending upon the context. In other words, **what is devoted or dedicated to God is accursed to man. If you keep back or steal God's property, then YOU become accursed.** (Hebrew "charam").

God's people were promised success, but only if they walked in obedience!

☑ **WHAT IS DEVOTED TO GOD IS ACCURSED TO MAN!**

A man named Achan did not obey and he took of the accursed things which were devoted to God. Because of this, the anger of the LORD burned against the children of Israel. By the way, the Hebrew word '**Akan** is from an unused root meaning "**to trouble**," or "**troublesome**." The LORD told Joshua that the man had stolen and deceived and put it among his own stuff. The LORD said, *"There is an accursed thing in your midst, O Israel; you cannot stand before your enemies until you take away the accursed thing from among you."* (Joshua 7:13)

Then the man, his sons, his daughters, his oxen, his donkeys, his sheep, his tent, and all that he had (including what he stolen that belonged to God) were burned with fire after the people of Israel stoned them with stones according to the command of the LORD.

This reminds us of Ananias and Sapphira who sold an estate, and kept back part of the proceeds, pretending to give ALL of it to the treasury of the church. They lied to the Holy Spirit and **both of them died within three hours of each other**. (Acts 5:1-11)

☑ NEVER LIE TO THE HOLY SPIRIT

These two examples above also remind us of God's promise in the book of Malachi.

"Will a man rob God? Yet you have robbed Me. But you say, 'In what way have we robbed You?' In tithes and offerings. You are cursed with a curse, for you have robbed Me, even this whole nation." (Malachi 3:8-9) Notice again, the beautiful purpose of this . . . and the LOVE of God . . . is shown in the following verses 10-11:

"Bring all the tithes into the storehouse that there may be food in My house, and PROVE ME now in this," says the LORD of hosts, ***"If I will not open for you the windows of Heaven, and pour you out such blessing that there will not be room enough to receive it."***

21

"And I will rebuke the devourer for your sakes, so that he will not destroy the fruit of your ground, nor shall the vine fail to bear fruit for you in the field ..." says the LORD of hosts.

NOTICE: God says you can PROVE Him . . . you can find out FOR SURE . . . God is Who He says He is: the great "I AM"—**by paying Him tithes and giving Him offerings!**

☑ **IF YOU ARE WILLING & OBEDIENT, YOU WILL EXPERIENCE VICTORY IN TRANSITION!**

The whole rest of your life you will be blessed as you follow these principles from God's Holy Word today. And, especially important to lay a foundation as you enter in to your next transition of creative prophecy for healing nations!

YOU HAVE NOT PASSED THIS WAY

Let me ask you some questions:

▮ What is the circumstance that is standing between you and your Promised Land?

▮ What is keeping you from attaining the Holy Spirit goals you have been praying for?

■ What is the lie the enemy keeps telling you that has kept you from entering in?

A NEW SEASON

After the children of Israel lodged for three days at the brink of the Jordan River, Joshua sent officers through the camp who commanded the people:

"When you see the ark of the covenant of the LORD your God, and the priests, the Levites, bearing it, then you shall set out from your place and go after it. Yet there shall be a space between you and the ark, about 2,000 cubits (1,000 yards or 914 meters) by measure. Do not come near the ark, that you may know the way by which you must go, for you have not passed this way before." [Joshua 3:1-4]

The Hebrew root word for **"passed"** used above is **"abar"** [ah-var] which means **"to pass over, go through, pass beyond, or to make a transition** [figuratively or literally]."

To arrive INSIDE your Promised Land, you will have to go through a TRANSITION! The Hebrew word "abar" also means **"to pass from one side to the other side."**

Interestingly enough, **a derivative of the word "abar"**

is "ibriy" which means "Hebrew" and is the **ethnic description of Abraham and his seed line**, who was **a descendant of Eber**, the great grandson of Noah's son, Shem.

In Genesis 14:13 we read about **"Abram the Hebrew."** Exodus 7:16 mentions **"the LORD God of the Hebrews."** Here "Hebrews" represents a tribe of Semites (sons of Shem).

Abraham "crossed over" the Euphrates River from Haran to Canaan, the land God promised him. How did he do it?—**through OBEDIENCE!** Abraham, his wife Sarah, and his nephew Lot had originally left Ur of the Chaldees with his father, Terah, and arrived in Haran. It's possible the LORD had wanted Terah to take the trip of faith from Haran and he may not have obeyed; possibly that is why God chose Abraham.

If you don't do it, God will find someone who will! Are you willing to make the transition from your comfort zone to a blessed place where millions of other people will be blessed by your life service or ministry?

The people of Israel were commanded to stay a great distance from the Ark as it would show them the way (verses 3 and 4). You are NOT to jump ahead of the LORD but to honor His holiness, just as the people honored the sacredness of the Ark. **Let God lead you—and then follow Him in faith**. He understands when you're not sure; but He also understands when you don't obey.

➡ **With your transition comes a NEW season!**

If your plans fit into God's plans …

You will have God's faith …

And God's faith always works!

Then, you can pass over and make the transition to the Promised Land: the completion of the Holy Spirit goals you have prayed for so long!

MIRACLES FOR YOUR TRANSITION

God sets up situations to bring you to the forefront of prophetic service to bring about healing of nations.

God works "behind the scenes" to bring mass deliverance of nations and groups of people—and God works for you! My friend, pray that God will guide you into the ministry of "national deliverance."

There are **many ways** God has to help you. Many times He or His angels are working ahead of time—or right on time—in unseen ways to deliver you, to prosper you, and to bring you into a place of super productivity.

We will now discuss more in detail how God works "behind the scenes" to bring mass deliverance of nations and groups of people. You will learn HOW to be an instrument God will use to impact the world, and even to open NEW, hitherto un-traversed frontiers.

Remember, God is FOR YOU. If you ever doubt this, look at the cross. If when we were His enemies He loved us so much that He sent His only unique Son to die for us, how much more, now that we are His friends, does He want to make us whole in every area of our lives. (Romans 5:10)

God has every detail of your life covered. If you walk in constant communion with Him—if the Holy Spirit is your best Friend—and if you are involved in kingdom work, then you can expect His VERY BEST for you.

"I will instruct you and teach you in the way you shall go; I will guide you with my eye." [Psalm 32:8]

Realize that this promise is both "individual" and "corporate". God is not only working for YOU, but also for those PEOPLE under your tutelage and leadership. He wants you to KNOW His deliverance, direction, and dynamics: for your sake—as well as the sake of those people under your watch care—and for the sake of people in the FUTURE!

Before Christopher Columbus (real name Cristobal

Colon) made his transatlantic voyages he began to believe that his plan for Atlantic navigation was divinely supported, that it was somehow connected with God's purpose for the world. Five pages of remnants of some of Columbus's original "papers" were sewn into the back of one of his favorite books: *Historia Revum Ubique Gestarum* or *History of All Things and All Deeds* by Aeneas Sylvius (later Pope Pius II), printed in Venice in 1477.

On one of these pages he had written the Old Testament books and prophets which inspired him. He wrote: "... the Holy Spirit, which with rays of marvelous brightness comforted me with His holy and sacred Scripture, in a high, clear voice." Surely, not all was perfect in his life, but he had been used as a marvelous vessel in frontier work that opened up the New World from which the Gospel and workers for Christ spread throughout the world in the last 500 years.

Also, think of the many people who have fled persecution and oppression through the centuries and found refuge in the New World. At the end of his life Columbus was convinced that prophecies had been fulfilled by his voyages to the Indies and he gave up his quest for science to *"cleave to the Holy and Sacred Scriptures."* I have used the life of Columbus as an example. You don't have to know every detail—and you don't have to be perfect—to be an instrument God will use to impact the world—and even to open NEW, hitherto un-traversed frontiers.

Let your heart speak to you.

Let the Spirit's prompting in your inner man guide you in accordance to the Holy Scriptures.

What is it that the Holy Spirit is leading you to implement? God's Spirit is in the business of impacting nations. He is in the business of opening NEW FRONTIERS. He works "behind the scenes" to bring mass deliverance of nations and groups of people. For those who will listen and pay the price, He births the ministry of "national deliverance".

A scripture generally ascribed to the end times tells us: *"And the gospel must first be published among all nations."* (Mark 13:10) The word for "nations" here is the Greek word "ethnos" which can mean a tribe or people with similar characteristics, or a race. It can be as broad as a nation and as narrow as a family or clan; and usually distinguished by linguistic or cultural characteristics.

God wants to impact clans and tribes, language groups and races ... people from all characteristic groups of the world to represent His Son's bride in Heaven.

"And they sung a new song, saying, You are worthy to take the book, and to open the seals thereof; for You were slain, and have redeemed us to God by your blood out of every kindred, and tongue, and people, and nation." (Revelation 5:9)

Q & A TIME

FIRST, how do you make this apply to yourself and life service or the ministry God has given you?

Answer: By identification with God's plan. If your plan fits into God's plan, you will have **God's faith** and God's faith **always** works!

SECOND, why would you want it to apply to you?

Answer: You will be able to effect tremendous and numerous MIRACLES—real miracles—of worldwide evangelization and church or synagogue planting with growth of disciples who are partaking in "strong meat".

THIRD, how can you implement this?

Answer: You will believe in faith for an **anointing of multiplication**.

When your heart is woven into the heart of God's plan then you can expect mighty DELIVERANCES as well as MIRACLES. God can work for you through many avenues:

- Enemies;
- Circumstances;
- Dreams or sleeplessness;
- Holy Angels;
- Fastings; and,
- Prayers of believers.

We see most, if not all, of the avenues listed above being used in the *Book of Esther.*

Ahasuerus was monarch of the Medo-Persian empire and ruled over 127 provinces from India to East Africa. He is generally believed to have been King Xerxes I who succeeded Darius I in 485 B.C. and ruled for 20 years. For six months He made a feast to all his princes and servants during which time he flaunted his riches. At the end of this time he made a great feast for seven days, inviting all people in Shushan, the palace. He had sent for his wife, Queen Vashti, to come that he might display her beauty to the crowd; but she refused, and the king became angry.

The king asked his wise men, the seven princes of Persia and Media: "What shall we do unto the Queen Vashti according to law, because she has not performed the commandment of King Ahasuerus by the household officers?" The consensus of the princes was that a decree should be made that every man should bear rule in his own house; and that Vashti could come no more before the king. Also, that her royal estate and position be given to another woman better than she.

Later, the king's servants that waited upon him suggested—and talked him into—making another decree: *"Let fair young virgins be sought for the king ... and let the maiden which pleases the king be replacement for Vashti."* (Esther 1:22-2:2) The king appointed officers in all 127 provinces of his kingdom to gather beautiful young virgins to the palace at Shushan so that he could choose one to be queen instead of Vashti.

TRANSITION TIME IN THE KINGDOM

In Shushan, the palace city of Persia, lived a Jew named Mordecai who had been taken captive from Jerusalem under Nebuchadnezzar, king of Babylon. Mordecai had raised his cousin, Esther, who was orphaned after her parents died. Esther was beautiful!

GOD SET THIS SITUATION UP TO BRING FORTH ESTHER AND MORDECAI GOD SETS SITUATIONS UP FOR YOU

Esther was ultimately chosen after at least 12 months of preparation with oil of myrrh and sweet aromas. (Esther 2:12) And the king loved Esther above all the women who were candidates to replace Vashti. She obtained *"grace and favor in his sight more than all the virgins; so he set the royal crown upon her head, and made her queen instead of Vashti."* (Esther 2:17) At this time Esther had not made known to the king that she was Jewish.

In those days Mordecai, Esther's cousin, found out that two of the king's officers were planning to assassinate the king. Mordecai told it to Esther the queen and she let the king know, also having the matter certified in the court records. These two men were then hanged.

After all these things the king promoted a man named Haman above all the princes in the kingdom, and the king commanded people to bow before Haman. **But Mordecai refused to do so, and told them that he was a Jew**. Eventually, people told Haman about this and he became full of anger. The people wanted to see if Mordecai would succeed; to see if there was any import to belonging to the God of Israel. Satan stirred up Haman and he then decided to destroy all the Jews, Mordecai's people, throughout the whole kingdom, from India to Ethiopia!

Haman lied to the king and convinced the king that the Jews were a bad influence in the kingdom and should be destroyed; he talked the king into letting Haman prepare a decree for their destruction in all 127 provinces. The copy of the decree was delivered by horsemen to the provinces ordering the massacre of all Jews, including women and children, on one set day and to take their material wealth.

GOD KNEW ABOUT HAMAN.

THE JEWS NEEDED DELIVERANCE.

GOD KNOWS ABOUT YOU.

HE KNOWS WHEN YOU NEED HELP.

In every province Jews started weeping and mourning; **many started fasting**. The Jews were not afraid to show their emotions; the time was drawing near for their extermination. Mordecai tore his clothes, put on sackcloth, and went out into middle of the city, crying

33

with a loud voice. Esther heard about Mordecai and sent one of the king's officers to find out what was happening.

GOD HONORS FASTING

WHEN IS THE LAST TIME YOU FASTED?
FAST TO PROTECT YOURSELF,
YOUR LOVED ONES & YOUR COUNTRY!

Mordecai showed the officer a copy of the decree that had been made, to show it to Esther, and to command her to go into the king to make request for mercy for her people, the Jews. But Esther sent the officer back to Mordecai to explain to him that she could not go into the king without having been called by him; **it was a death sentence to do so**. Also, she had not been called by the king for the last 30 days.

But Mordecai answered her back: *"Don't think that you will escape in the king's house more than all the Jews. For if you altogether hold you peace at this time, then there shall ENLARGEMENT and DELIVERANCE [from God] arise to the Jews from another place; but you and your father's house shall be destroyed; and* **who** *knows whether you have come to the kingdom for such a time as this?"* [Esther 4:14]

God brings deliverance **AND** enlargement. **When He delivers you from something He then provides enlargement.**

WHEN GOD DELIVERS YOU
HE ALSO PROVIDES ENLARGEMENT

King David said, *"He brought me forth also into **a large place**; He delivered me, because he delighted in me."* [2 Samuel 22:20 and Psalm 18:19]

After God delivered Israel from Egypt he directed them to **a LARGE place** of NO WANT. *"When you go, you shall come unto a people secure, and to **a large land**: for God has given it into your hands; a place **where there is no want** of anything that is in the earth."* (Judges 18:10)

Then Esther sent an answer back to Mordecai saying, *"Go gather together all the Jews that are present in Shushan and fast for me; and don't eat or drink for three days, night or day. I, also, and my maidens will fast the same. I will go in unto the king, which is not according to the law, and if I die, I die."* (Verses 15 and 16)

YOUR DECISION TO DIE TO *YOUR* WILL
BRINGS YOU INTO TRANSITION

Yeshua (Jesus) taught, *"For whosoever will save his life shall lose it: but whosoever will lose his life for my sake, the same shall save it."* (Luke 9:24)

On the third day of complete fasting, Esther went into the inner court of the king's house and stood before him while he was on his throne. She obtained favor in his sight and he held out his golden scepter to her. The king asked her what she wanted; that it would be given her to the half of his kingdom. She then invited the king— and Haman—to a banquet she had prepared that day.

NEVER LET YOUR ENEMY KNOW
WHAT YOU'RE PLANNING

At the banquet the king asked her what her request was. She then invited the king—and Haman—to a second banquet she would have the next day and told the king she would then make her request known.

NOTICE THE IMPORTANCE OF TIMING
—AND—
OF BEING LED BY THE SPIRIT OF GOD

After this first banquet, Haman went home happy but as he passed the king's gate Mordecai would not bow down to him. This made Haman mad but he restrained himself. At home, he told his wife Zeresh and his friends about his promotion and the invitation he received to the banquet the next day. Also, he told them about passing Mordecai in the king's gate and that Mordecai would not bow down to him.

Haman's wife and friends told him he should build a gallows 75 feet high (about 23 meters) upon which to hang Mordecai, and that he should ask the king for permission to do the same the next day at the banquet. That made Haman happy and he caused the gallows to be made.

THE NEXT 24 HOURS WERE OF CRITICAL IMPORTANCE TO ESTHER AND THE JEWS.

WHAT ABOUT THE NEXT 24 HOURS IN YOUR LIFE AND IN YOUR COUNTRY?

That night the king could not sleep and he commanded someone to read the records (chronicles) of the kingdom. Written in the records he found that Mordecai had saved him from an assassination attempt; and he asked, *"What honor and dignity has been done to Mordecai for this?"* His servants answered, *"Nothing has been done for him."*

AN ANGEL KEPT THE KING AWAKE. GOD WAS ANSWERING THE PRAYERS AND THE FASTING OF THE JEWS.

About then Haman came into the outer court to speak to the king about hanging Mordecai. The king asked Haman, *"What shall be done to the man whom the king delights to honor?"* Thinking the king was talking about himself (Haman), Haman answered, *"Put* *royal clothes of the king upon him, with the royal crown, and let him ride through the city on the king's horse."* **Then the king commanded Haman to do this to Mordecai.**

Before it was time to go to the second banquet of Esther's, Haman went home mourning (because of Mordecai's success). Even his wife and friends told him, *"If Mordecai be of the seed of the Jews, before whom you have begun to fall, you shall not prevail against him, but shall surely fall before him."* (Esther 6:13)

NEVER PUT YOUR HAND AGAINST THE JEWS OR AGAINST ISRAEL

"And I will bless them that bless you, and curse him that curses you: and in you shall all families of the earth be blessed." (Genesis 12:3)

While Haman and his wife were still talking, the king's officer came to take Mordecai to the second banquet Esther had prepared. **At the banquet, Esther told the king her petition**. She told him of the plans to destroy her people, the Jews, and that wicked Haman was the adversary. Then one of the king's servants told the king about the gallows Haman had prepared upon which he planned to hang Mordecai. The king said, *"Hang him (Haman) thereon."* [Esther 7:9]

On that day the king gave the house of Haman, the Jews enemy, to Queen Esther. **Esther told the king that Mordecai was her cousin and that he had raised her after the death of her parents**. The king took off his ring (which he had taken from Haman) and gave it to Mordecai. **Esther then set Mordecai over the house of Haman**.

The king then told Esther and Mordecai to write a decree allowing the Jews in every province from Ethiopia to India to protect themselves and to destroy all who would attempt to harm them. They were also given permission to take plunder and take goods from their enemies.

DON'T QUIT TOO SOON

The king told Esther that the Jews had destroyed 500 men in Shushan and the ten sons of Haman. **Esther then made a second request**: that the Jews could attack their enemies the next day, also; and she asked that the dead bodies of Haman's sons be hanged from the gallows he had prepared for Mordecai. This request was granted.

Approximately 75,800 of the Jews enemies were killed in the 127 provinces, **but the Jews did NOT take any of their enemy's goods**.

Mordecai became second in the kingdom, next to the king, and great among the Jews, and accepted of the multitude of his brethren, seeking the wealth of his people, and speaking peace to all his seed.

Esther is enumerated by the Rabbis as one of the seven women prophets of Israel. (BT Megillah 14a) She spoke creative prophetic decrees that influenced a whole nation of people—the Jews—and influenced 127 provinces from India to Ethiopia.

THE DEVIL HATES ISRAEL AND THE JEWS

First, because it was through the Jewish seed line that Messiah Yeshua was born. Second, the Jews are close to God's heart: they are God's chosen people.

"For thou art a holy people unto the LORD thy God: the LORD thy God has chosen thee to be a special people unto himself, above all people that are upon the face of the earth." (Deuteronomy 7:6)

"For the LORD did not set his love upon you, nor choose you, because you were more in number than any people, for you were the fewest of all people. But [you were chosen] because the LORD loved you, and because he would keep the oath which he had sworn unto your fathers ..." (Deuteronomy 7:7-8)

The devil showed his hatred of the Jews in Nazi Germany when he had 6,000,000 killed under Adolph Hitler.

SATAN TRIED THIS MANY TIMES
HE DID NOT WANT MESSIAH BORN

■ The enemy tried to destroy the Hebrew boys in Moses' day under Pharaoh.

■ The enemy tried to destroy the Hebrew boys in Esther's day under Haman.

■ The enemy tried to destroy the Hebrew boys in Jesus' day under King Herod.

SATAN WILL TRY AGAIN TO DESTROY THE JEWS. HE DOES NOT WANT THE MESSIAH TO RETURN THE SECOND TIME TO ESTABLISH HIS KINGDOM.

The devil will try to destroy the Jews with a cataclysmic flood during the Great Tribulation. (Revelation 12:13-17) The devil KNOWS that when the Jews INVITE the Messiah back—then He will return!

"And I will pour out upon the house of David, and upon the inhabitants of Jerusalem, the spirit of grace and of supplications, and they shall look upon me whom they have pierced, and they shall mourn for him, as one mourns for his only son, and shall be in bitterness for Him, as one that is in bitterness for his firstborn." (Zechariah 12:9)

"In that day there shall be a fountain opened to the house of David and to the inhabitants of Jerusalem for sin and for uncleanness." (Zechariah 13:1)

Ask God for the prophetic office of "national deliverance". You can be instrumental in the impact of the Holy Spirit upon your country or region, upon Israel, and upon your family, tribe, or ethnic group.

Who knows whether you have come to the kingdom for such a time as this?!

You can be a prophetic instrument of transition and MIRACLES: for yourself ... and for others!

TRANSITION WITH MIRACLES

Joshua was Moses' Chief aide and military leader; he became Israel's leader after Moses' death. Joshua led the people across the Jordan and into the promised land.

Seven (7) nations were destroyed in the land. After the conquest of the land by the children of Israel, the land was divided among the tribes of Israel.

There were tremendous MIRACLES in Joshua's day:

- The crossing of Jordan
- The fall of Jericho
- The sun standing still.

NOTE: **All these miracles had to do with getting God's people into the land and driving out the enemy!** They were involved in God's plan and purpose to reach the world for Messiah! **If you're involved in God's PLAN and PURPOSE to reach the world for**

Messiah Jesus, God will do GREAT MIRACLES for and through you!

Remember: The KEY to the Old Testament: "A record of a nation designed to bring forth a Man (the Messiah of God)." The KEY of the New Testament is: "A record of a Man (the Messiah of God) designed to bring forth a nation (the people of God)."

"For this purpose the Son of God was manifested, that He might destroy the works of the devil." – I John 3:8

Your job is the same as Joshua's. To go into new territory and conquer for the Lord; to destroy the works of the devil; and then to divide the land (inheritance) among God's people.

To conquer for the LORD completely and successfully you have to **KNOW your authority in Christ**. You have to **believe ALL the teachings of Jesus**. This **includes His validation of a 24 hour day in Creation** —a young earth, and NOT billions of years in evolutionary process—**and that He is a Baptizer (in the Holy Spirit)** as well as a Savour, a Healer, a Deliverer, and a King.

To conquer for the LORD completely and successfully you also have to believe that **the Holy Bible is the inspired Word of God in entirety** and NOT just the text of God's Word. Textual criticism—*form geschicte or form criticism*—(Christian) evolutionary hypothesis—*including other more recent speculations of scriptural* *historical revelation and recordation*—**will never earn you the right to a MIRACLE sign gifted ministry.** Conversely, they will ROB you—*cheat you*—of the power of God.

Now you realize why you do NOT see so many MIRACLES—real miracles—in churches or in the graduate seminaries that are churning out pastors. I have been a student at several seminaries and **the only time I ever witnessed MIRACLES was at the University of Judaism**, where all my instructors were Israeli. There the LORD used me to give signs to His wonderful Jewish people.

There is NO major MIRACLE ministry in the earth today that does NOT believe:

1. In a 24 hour literal day for the Creation record in Genesis;

2. That the Holy Bible is the inspired inerrant Word of God in entirety; and,

3. That Jesus still wants to heal and do miracles today.

You might ask, "How do I divide the land among God's people?" Here's your answer: **By teaching them their authority in Christ—WHO they are in Christ and WHAT they have in Christ—by teaching them HOW you conquered, and sharing the blessings you have received, so they will know how to conquer: HOW TO WIN!**

Do you have your orders from God like Moses and Joshua? Are you operating in the perfect center of God's will for your life? If not, PRAY, and ask God to show you His plan for your life. Spend time ALONE with God daily in your prayer closet (a regular place where you can meet with Him). If your plan fits into God's plan, you will have God's faith: and God's faith always works!

READ IT AGAIN:

If your plan fits into God's plan ...
you will have God's faith ...
and God's faith always works!

TO TRANSITION, FOLLOW GOD'S ADVICE

Moses led over 3,000,000 people through the wilderness. Multiply the male census (603,550) by 2 (allowing each man a wife) = 1,200,000 and then figure 3 children (minimum) for every family (3 X 600,000 = 1,800,000).

Whenever a major problem arose, he prayed and talked to God about it before he took action.

The one time he acted foolishly—when he did not take God's advice—cost him earthly blessings. He became angry so that he "hit" the rock instead of "speaking" to it. Forty years before, God had told him to "hit" the rock and water would come out for the people to drink.

However, near the end of the wilderness wanderings, when the people were complaining over thirst again, God told him only to SPEAK to the rock and water would come out. Moses became angry and, even though the fault was with the people he was leading, the Bible says: "*he spoke **unadvisedly** with his lips*". He called them a bunch of rebels. Read Exodus 17:1-7; Numbers 20:1-13; and Psalm 106:32-33.

SPEAK PROPHETICALLY – NOT RASHLY.

IN TRANSITION, FOLLOW GOD'S ADVICE.

MIRACLES WILL FOLLOW YOU.

Make sure YOUR PLAN fits into GOD'S PLAN.

Seek God's advice and follow it.

Teach people their authority in Christ.
Divide the land among God's people.

**If your plan fits into God's plan ...
you will have God's faith ...
and God's faith always works!**

*"You shall also decree a thing, and it shall be
established unto you: and the light shall shine
upon your ways." – Job 22:28*

YOUR NEXT TRANSITION

Do not be afraid of doing the wrong **right** thing!

Listen to God and make a decision!

When I was a little boy, about 11 years of age, **I
prophesied that men would travel to the moon**. No
one ever dreamed, or talked about, such a thing
happening. I also prophesied that I would serve God
when I grew up. The latter was probably more of a long
shot statistically than the former (at least to those who
knew me). Many years later both prophecies came to
pass. Think **BIG** and prophesy **BIG** when you **know** it
is God.

What stirs you? What makes you come to life? Spend
time in the Word of God. When you do, things will
begin to click in your life. God will provide for you and
you will be productive.

Change your thinking! Do not limit yourself by your own thoughts!

THINK BIG

BELIEVE

RECEIVE

ACT

MULTIPLY

COMMISSION

Remember the acronym: **T**rue **B**lood **R**an **A**t Mount **C**alvary.

God is NOT old; He is eternally young. He is NOT limited, even by your disobedience. In 2 Kings Chapter 7 we see the productivity and success of **anointed common sense**. There was a famine in the land. Also, the Syrian army laid siege to the Israelites in this area. Four (4) lepers were outside the city gates. They were facing death because of famine, just like the other people. But they were also vexed with an incurable disease: leprosy. The king and other people would not allow them to come into the city.

On a certain day the four lepers said to one another, *"Why are we sitting here until we die? If we say, We will enter the city, the famine is in the city, and we shall die there. And if we sit here, we die also. Now therefore, come, let us surrender to the army of the Syrians. If they keep us alive, we shall live; and if they kill us, we shall only die."*

When they came to the outskirts of the Syrian camp, to their surprise **no one was there**. For the LORD had caused the army of the Syrians to hear the noise of chariots and the noise of horses—the noise of a great army; so they (the Syrians) said to one another, *"Look, the king of Israel has hired against us the kings of the Hittites and the kings of the Egyptians to attack us."*

Therefore the Syrians arose at twilight and fled; they left everything in their camp intact: food, silver, gold, clothing, tents, horses, and donkeys. They even threw away their weapons as they fled.

In 24 hours the economy changed … literally overnight. **It had been prophesied by Elisha the day before** (2 Kings 7:1). God found four lepers who had **spiritual common sense**. As soon as the lepers made a **MOVE**, God caused the Syrians to hear the sound of a great army.

THERE ARE THINGS **IN YOUR LIFE** THAT WILL NEVER HAPPEN UNTIL YOU USE **SPIRITUAL COMMON SENSE** AND **TRANSITION** IN FAITH.

IF YOU ARE DYING SPIRITUALLY WHERE YOU ARE AT—IF YOU ARE NOT PRODUCTIVE—THEN **USE SPIRITUAL COMMON SENSE** AND **TRANSITION** AFTER YOU HAVE HEARD FROM GOD.

You may be in a situation now very similar to that of the four lepers. You are perishing spiritually where you are. That is, your life is not as productive as God wants it to be. You want BIG things to happen in your life: to reach people around the world for Messiah Jesus.

Take a step of faith—**TRANSITION**—into the area which God is showing you.

What do you have to lose? Read the Word of God and **listen**. Talk to Him and LISTEN. Pray in tongues and LISTEN. **Then do what He tells you**.

Decree prophetically. Create prophetically.

Jesus said, *"The field is the world."* (Matthew 13:38-43) Jesus also taught that if YOU want to get the treasure out of the field, you have to **buy the WHOLE FIELD**. (Matthew 13:44) If you want to reach China, then you have to purchase the whole field. If you want to reach Iran, then you have to purchase the whole field. **Meditate on this!**

Nothing happened until the four lepers made the **TRANSITION** in the right direction.

Nothing happened until the priests of Israel made the **TRANSITION** and put their feet in the River Jordan.

When you **TRANSITION** out of obedient faith—then the

God of Israel will cause things to happen. He will make a way for you!

This will be your next important transition—don't miss it!

Do not be afraid of doing the wrong **right** thing!

The destiny of ethnic and people groups is hanging in the balance.

Lay your left hand on your head and lay your right hand upon your heart and repeat these three (3) words:

NATIONS ... NATIONS ... NATIONS!

PROPHETIC DECREES AND MIRACLES

We are at a turning point for the Body of Messiah. God is dealing in the earth—in nations, regions and ideologies—to prepare workers in Messianic Synagogues and Holy Spirit Power Churches, readying them and placing them into position for the Great Harvest before the coming of the LORD.

Ministers of God who have been faithfully serving behind the scenes will now begin to emerge to the forefront. It will be a forefront—not of pride—but a leading position of effectiveness: a place of UNIQUE and OVERWHELMING INFLUENCE to the nations of the world. This influence will begin to flow into the leaders of every strata of society, and then from these leaders this Spirit anointed influence will emanate to their respective circles of influence.

Many of you reading this book will be affected by this move—and many will **transition into a prophetic–healing ministry**. To be **faithful** to this calling, you must first **listen** to God. This presupposes that:

■ You daily spend time in God's Word.

■ You daily spend time in your private place of prayer and intercession.

■ You live holy.

■ You harbor NO unforgiveness towards any person, ministry, or church.

■ You fast as the Holy Spirit leads you.

The above are mandatory for all true ministry giftings, not just the prophetic office. You must have a **platform** to stand upon. From such a platform, God will create other platforms of **confidence for ministry** created via His Word.

Satan will try to spawn lies about some of you and use loved ones, as well as fellow ministers, to spread these attacks of deception. Forgive them and pray for them. For whatever reason they take part in these rumors, **they will pay a great price**. You will not need to fight in this battle, for *"the battle is the LORD's."* **You will ultimately be cleared of these attacks and those who have participated will come to you for forgiveness, or receive more severe judgment**.

Many of you reading this teaching will be affected by this move—and **many will transition into a prophetic-healing ministry**. You will know if this is YOU as God will already have given you **waymarks** along the way that—if you haven't recognized them already—you will now be able to look back and SEE, with spiritual eyesight, how they have been placed in your life.

Emails that have come to me as a result of a teaching I made titled, *The Vision God Gave Me*, has prompted me to share about **how prophecy and visions may come**. Sometimes they may come infrequently, over a period of months or years; other times, frequently.

As I mentioned previously, when I was 11 years of age I gave a DOUBLE prophecy at the same time to my older sister and a neighbor who was in our dining room. I remember the exact spot. **I told them that men would one day travel to the moon** (this was many years before such exploration had even been pondered) and, also, that I would one day serve God. Both came to pass! I loved Jesus at that age and won a

Bible for inviting 17 kids to my Sunday School class, but after my father died four years later I wandered into sin. Praise God, I gave my life to Messiah Jesus after graduating from the first college I attended.

Starting in the early 1970's I prophesied several times that God was going to elevate Holy Spirit baptized African Americans into positions of political leadership. This came to pass after several years.

At times, the Lord would give me **specific prophecies** (not words of knowledge) for specific individuals. For example, one man who had been involved politically and who was an attorney, had dedicated his life to ministry. Yet, he had not experienced an answer to what he had received as a vision for God's will for him. After a few years, I was speaking in a city where he had moved, and met him again. We had lunch together and I prophesied to him: **"You will receive an offer for employment in ministry within 24 hours."** It came to pass, and he was exceedingly happy. (No, I had nothing to do with it, nor any knowledge of it!)

After teaching at a seminar at McCormick Place in Chicago, USA, a lady came up to me and asked me for a word of prophecy. I was really wanting to go my room because I had ministered quite late and prayed for the sick. I think she was the last person I talked to. She told me: *"I have two wombs. If I conceive in the one womb, the baby will live; if I conceive in the other, it will die. Do you have a word for me?"* **I prophesied to her instantly, and said: "You will have a son. His name will be Samuel, and he will live."**

About two years or so later I was in that area ministering again. The lady came up to me afterwards (I had forgotten about her or who she was), and invited me to her home for dinner the next day. I went, met her husband who was a policeman, and **then she brought out little Samuel**, and reminded me of the prophecy!

Healing many time accompanies prophecy. And, more specifically, **a word of healing** will accompany prophecy, **similar to a word of knowledge.** For example, one time in Houston, Texas **I prayed for several barren ladies who could not have children. I prophesied to them and laid hands on them. Every one of them conceived within 30 days!** Interestingly enough, the next time I was in that city, women were saying to me, *"Don't lay hands on me!"*

At times I have laid hands on people in meetings and prophesied **"Nations, nations, nations!"** and specifically, **"You will preach to crowds of tens of thousands."** One time several ministers were at a convention, and as they got up **one by one** to testify they discovered that I had laid hands on each one of them and prophesied the same about nations, and that **ALL of the prophecies had come to pass specifically.** One minister had been ready to quit pastoring, and then began to preach to crowds of tens

57

of thousands. Praise God for speaking to the hearts of His people to bless them and then bring salvation and healing to multitudes.

What I am prophesying to you today is this:

> *We are at a turning point for the Body of Messiah. God is dealing in the earth to prepare workers in the Body of Messiah, readying them and placing them into position for the Great Harvest before the coming of the LORD.*
>
> *Ministers and workers of God who have been faithfully serving behind the scenes will now emerge to the forefront. It will be a forefront—not of pride—but a leading position of effectiveness:* ***a place of UNIQUE and OVERWHELMING INFLUENCE to the nations of the world.*** *This influence will begin to flow into the leaders of every strata of society, and then from these leaders this Spirit anointed influence will emanate to their respective circles of influence.*
>
> *Many of you reading this prophecy will be affected by this move—and many will transition into a prophetic-healing ministry.*

Healing is so important. If you haven't already, ready and study the book, *Health and Healing Complete*

Guide to Wholeness. (Available at Amazon and other book stores.)

Also, memorize the scriptures in the book, *Total Person Toolbox*, available at Amazon and other book stores.

When Jesus was on the cross He cried out to the Father, *"My God, my God, why have you forsaken me?"* He was in such pain for YOU and for ME and for the sins of ALL PEOPLE. **He bore our sins, sicknesses, diseases, and pains**—so we would **not** have to bear them. (Isaiah Chapter 53 – Tanakh, Hebrew scriptures.)

Jesus was resurrected—you will be, too. **Go pray for the sick**. Promise God you will start the **prophetic–healing ministry** to which He is calling you. Pray for God to give you a **specific healing word** for people. All Christians who are baptized in the Holy Spirit have the authority to heal the sick, and if you are operating in the prophetic, **you have the anointing to prophesy— within the confines of the Word of God—specific healing words**.

➡ The same applies to **prophetically decreed—** *creative*—**prophecy** directed to **national deliverance**.

➡ The same applies to **speaking confusion and frustration into evil empires**, groups and people that seek to harm peaceful people and nations. [Such as **ISIS and other terrorist factions** and entities.]

➡ The same applies to **prophetic decrees for the release of dreams and visions** into the ethnic groups bound in false religion and darkness.

Let me give you some examples. I held a training seminar in San Diego, California (USA) for ministers from other countries. There were men there who were ex-Muslims. Two of the pastors in that seminar—who were NOT from the same area—**had the exact same testimony**.

They both had had two weeks to live due to disease. The LORD **Jesus appeared to each man** separately—the men did NOT know each other—and said these exact words to each of them: *"If I heal you … will you serve me?"*

Both of the men said, *"Yes"* to Jesus … and **both were healed miraculously**. One of those men I had the privilege to ordain in the ministry. He had already started 32 churches.

Many Muslims are being saved due to Jesus appearing to them in dreams, visions or in person. You can **release the supernatural through the agency of prophetic decrees** initiated by FAITH based upon God's Holy Word. It is the will of God for those in darkness to be saved—that's WHY the Father sent His Son: Jesus.

DECREE FOR ESTABLISHMENT

This is where the POINT OF DECISION is so important. **Learn to ACT towards God at the point of decision.** My mother used to say, *"You should have nipped it in the bud."* We are continuously growing forests: either negatively or positively. This is why Jesus said: *"For a beautiful tree does not produce worthless fruit; neither does a rotten tree produce valuable fruit."* (Luke 6:43) We are not just planting forests when we give money. We are continuously growing forests—**positive forests or negative forests**—good forests or bad forests! *"Be not deceived; God is not mocked: for whatsoever a man sows, that shall he also reap."* (Galatians 6:7)

Jesus also instructed us: *"For from within, out of the heart of men, proceed evil thoughts, adulteries, fornications, murders, thefts, covetousness, wickedness, deceit, lasciviousness, an evil eye, blasphemy, pride, foolishness: **all these things come from within,** and defile the man."* (Mark 7:21-23) This is why the Proverbs admonish us, **"For as a person thinks in his heart, so is he."** (Proverb 23:7)

In Job 22:28 we read, **"You shall also decree a thing, and it shall be established unto you ..."** In the original Hebrew language the word "decree" is a primitive root form of the word "gazar", which means **"to cut out exclusively, or to decide"**. In its primitive form it is used also as a "quarrying" term—as in cutting

61

out stone from a rock quarry. It means more than to "say" or "speak." **It conveys the meaning of "cutting something out in your mind's eye"**; that is, "to envision—**to make a vision—to decide upon it**, and confess it"—and then it will be established unto you!

Learn to control your heart—your inner thought processes! **Your inner thought processes are constantly planting NEW FORESTS that will either grow to advantage or disadvantage—for you, for others, for nations**. This is one reason the Bible says in 1 Corinthians 13 that *"love—believes all things, hopes all things."* (Verse 7)

Faith works through love (Galatians 5:6). **So we first must have a vehicle (or, a conduit) through which our faith can work**. I have heard people spouting words of faith who at the same time didn't seem to be emanating much love. We, at times—especially in difficult situations—have to back up one step and ASK God for love. Then, we can believe all things, hope all things. **Then, we can grow large quality forests—and tear down large destructive works!**

How many times have you had a thought that played out? Maybe it was something good that you really wanted—or maybe it was something you were afraid of. I was talking to a person on the phone recently who was not a believer and who said to me, *"Whenever I have a thought about something it happens to me."*

Learn to spend quality time meditating and thinking —visualizing in the mind's eye of your heart—the **GREAT THINGS you want to do for God**. Plant and grow GIANT FORESTS of good. Remember, God promised you that He is *"able to do exceeding abundantly above all that you ask or think."* (Ephesians 3:20)

Spend time planting and cultivating **creative prophecy**. Any worthwhile thing in life takes time, so why not spend good quality time planning and preparing **national deliverance for people and empires—kingdom transition—with MIRACLES**.

There are several practical keys to growing GOOD forests. **These KEYS are effective in bringing about national deliverance.** Let me suggest three (3) to help you:

- **DECIDE** what kind of forest you want.
  - The kind of lumber you want to grow.
  - The location of the forest.

- **SEE** the forest.

- **ACT** on the vision with creative prophecy.

INTEL FOR PROPHETS

The office of Prophet is a KEY tactical spiritual position, and one that is extremely dangerous to Satan and his dark kingdom and workers. Therefore, the enemy tries to tempt, disillusion and discourage the real prophets of God. **I am going to reveal to you HOW to make sure this does NOT happen to YOU**.

Not only is **national deliverance** a prime threat to the enemy, but also the **influence of MIRACLES** in key centers of commerce and governmental influence. In this section of the book you will learn prophetic intel for your protection and to sharpen your discernment. You can't fight a war effectively unless you know what types of warfare your enemy may utilize.

We can't just resign ourselves to the fact that the LORD will flush everything out after the Battle of Armageddon. Our job—our responsibility—is to **fight an effective, ongoing and victorious, battle** so that the maximum number of people, including Jews, have opportunity to come into the Kingdom. Also, that we war in the Spirit—**by creative prophetic decrees**—to provide nations and people groups MIRACLES that will provide a spiritual climate for them to receive Messiah Jesus.

We previously discussed the importance of the POINT OF DECISION. In this section of the book we will discuss the contradistinction of growing GOOD forests, and teach you how to prevent bad forests: forests that wreck lives, families, and ministries. **Preparation ahead of time is invaluable because your enemy is already, and always, planning for your demise**. In this teaching I am going to provide you with **revealed knowledge** upon which you may act, and thereby enable you to successfully resist the devil and prevent bad forests from growing.

First of all, let me say that the Word of God teaches us to *"Resist the devil, and he will flee from you."* (James 4:7) However—in the forerunner of the last days in which we live—the enemy has many tricks with which both to allure and deceive you **to attempt to position you in a state of spiritual lethargy**: so that you will be caught in his trap and not want to resist —until it's too late.

He may attack you unwittingly at first in a dream, through an advertisement, in a medium of entertainment—or in thought. He knows that you know the Word of God. **The enemy has to work through BOTH your mind and your senses**.

We previously discussed growing GOOD forests through your thinking, your ideas, and even your attitudes. We also discussed that you can grow BAD forests. This is where the **POINT OF DECISION** is so important. Study again prayerfully "Growing Good Forests" under the section *Decree for Establishment*. It is extremely important!

When you have a good idea, other things many times interrupt you. Why do you think this happens? Usually, it is none other than the work of Satan. Let me explain—through revealed knowledge revealed to me by the Holy Spirit—how the enemy works upon you. The devil is like a man who takes advantage of a woman, and then leaves her. He takes advantage of you by tempting you with an idea. **You SEE the idea. Your carnal man then wants, or desires, to be involved in the WRONG action: the implementation of the BAD idea**.

After the WRONG or BAD activity is initiated and then consummated, the following things happen:

> The anointing of the Holy Spirit leaves you;
>
> The devil leaves you;***
>
> False peace enters; and then,
>
> Conviction enters (an awareness that something is wrong).

***NOTICE: **The devil will not leave you (that is, stop badgering you) until the anointing leaves you**. That's why people then have a false sense of peace. They are NOT any longer experiencing the drive and temptation of the enemy. (He doesn't need to bother them at this juncture, because he finished his job: to get them to lose the anointing.) This doesn't mean they don't have the Holy Spirit in them, or that they can't win souls, witness, or minister—it means they have ceased being a "new sharp threshing instrument" in Kingdom work—**the anointing is gone**. Samson didn't have the Holy Spirit IN him, but he had the anointing of the Spirit **upon him** for service until he lost it. King David cried out, after he had sinned, *"... take not your Holy Spirit from me."*

This is why the POINT OF DECISION is so important. **As soon as you have a BAD IDEA, do the following**:

1. Resist the devil with the Word of God. (James 4:7)

2. If the drawing of Satan (the temptation) is too strong, you MUST take the "way of escape" immediately. This is because the enemy has already gained a foothold in your mind and or senses.

> *"There has no temptation taken you but such as is common to man, but God is faithful, who will not suffer you to be tempted above that which you are able (to withstand); but will with the temptation also make a way of escape, that you may be able to bear it."*
>
> – 1 Corinthians 10:13

You MUST WANT to take the "way of escape." My job in this teaching is to reveal to you—with the help of the Holy Spirit—HOW MUCH Satan hates you and wants to ruin your life, your family and your ministry. **The devil does NOT want you to be a powerful prophetic instrument for God.** You need to SEE THIS FACT. You can give the devil NO PLACE from which he may operate or attack you. The enemy is really trying to attack God and His Kingdom through you diffusing your influence and power.

This is why—if you will read the context of the passage in Corinthians—the Spirit says in the previous verse: *"Wherefore let him that thinks he stand take heed lest he fall."* (Verse 12)

The temptation may be to do anything contrary to the will of God. (The Word of God is the WILL of God.) The temptation may be in any form. The enemy knows where you are most vulnerable. **Once you have learned to protect yourself in these areas, he will try to devise NEW MEANS to attack you: new ideas to allure you**.

3. Immediately, get on your knees and cry out to God to deliver you. The scripture says, *"And call upon me in the day of trouble: I will deliver you, and you shall glorify me."* (Psalm 50:15)

The POINT OF DECISION is where you have to act— **you have to move toward God**. The enemy is called "the serpent" because he is slithery and deadly. Many Christians—some of them leaders, anointed by God— have lost the anointing and grown bad forests. They thought they could stand, and let down their guard.

You and I are in a war which comprises many and continuous spiritual battles. **Our Commander-in-Chief has promised us victory if we listen to His directives**. My purpose in this teaching is to remind you of how vicious the enemy is, and how he will try to subtly attack you just like he did Eve in the garden. The enemy will use three (3) areas of attack:

■ The lust of the flesh—**appetite**—the taste (good for food).

■ The lust of the eyes—**appeal**—good to look upon.

■ The pride of life—**applause**—the desire to make one wise.

The Apostle John wrote: *"Love not the world, neither the things that are in the world. If any person loves the world, the love of the Father is not in him. For all that is in the world—**the lust of the flesh, the lust of the eyes, and the pride of life**—is not of the Father, but is of the world. And the world passes away, and the lust thereof; but he that does the will of God abides forever."* (1 John 2:15-17)

"Commit your works to the LORD and your thoughts will be established." (Proverbs 16:3) **The Master has need of you**. Do NOT let somebody be hurt—and do NOT let your Savior be hurt—as a result of your growing BAD forests.

The POINT OF DECISION is where you have to act. Grow GOOD large and productive forests—**with creative prophetic decrees**—for your family, your community and the nations of the world ... and for yourself!

Now you know the secret of **Prophecy, Transition and Miracles**.

Have a wonderful life serving God in the prophetic office. May His grace abound more and more as you transition and bring deliverance to nations, MIRACLE healing to people—and as you progress on your journey to Heaven, showing other people the Way.

Here's a promise for YOU. I have seen many MIRACLES claiming this promise from GOD:

"Call to me and I will answer you, and show you great and mighty things which you do not know."
– Tanakh: Jeremiah 33:3

LIVE A LIFE OF EXCELLENCE!

OTHER BOOKS BY PRINCE HANDLEY

- Map of the End Times
- How to Do Great Works
- Flow Chart of Revelation
- Action Keys for Success
- Health and Healing Complete Guide to Wholeness
- Prophetic Calendar for Israel & the Nations: Thru 2023
- Healing Deliverance
- How to Receive God's Power with Gifts of the Spirit
- Healing for Mental and Physical Abuse
- Victory Over Opposition and Resistance
- Healing of Emotional Wounds
- How to Be Healed and Live in Divine Health
- Healing from Fear, Shame and Anger
- How to Receive Healing and Bring Healing to Others
- New Global Strategy: Enabling Missions
- The Art of Christian Warfare
- Success Cycles and Secrets
- New Testament Bible Studies (A Study Manual)
- Babylon the Bitch – Enemy of Israel
- Resurrection Multiplication – Miracle Production
- Faith and Quantum Physics – Your Future
- Conflict Healing – Relational Health
- Decision Making 101 – Know for Sure
- Total Person Toolbox

AVAILABLE AT AMAZON AND OTHER BOOK STORES
UNIVERSITY OF EXCELLENCE PRESS

BONUS

To help you, and to help you teach others, we have prepared Rabbinical Studies at this site:

www.uofe.org/RABBINICAL_STUDIES.html

These are commentaries from **ancient** Jewish Rabbis that identify the Mashiach of Israel.

To help you, and to help you teach others, we have also prepared Bible Studies in English, Spanish and French.

- English FREE Bible Studies

  www.uofe.org/english_bible_studies.html

- Spanish FREE Bible Studies

  www.uofe.org/spanish_bible_studies.html

- French FREE Bible Studies

  www.uofe.org/french_bible_studies.html

ANNOUNCEMENT

We recommend you study the following companion books in the **Prophecy Series** to help in your journey of Prophecy, Transitions and Miracles.

- *Map of the End Times.*

- *Flow Chart of Revelation.*

- *Babylon the Bitch – Enemy of Israel.*

- *Prophetic Calendar for Israel and the Nations*

Books are available at Amazon and other book stores.

✝

NOTE

We listen to our readers. Tell us what **new** subject matter you would like to see published. Email your ideas to: universityofexcellence@gmail.com.

UNIVERSITY OF EXCELLENCE PRESS
Los Angeles ■ London ■ Tel Aviv

NOTE

We listen to our readers. Tell us what **new** subject matter you would like to see published. Email your ideas to: universityofexcellence@gmail.com.

www.ingramcontent.com/pod-product-compliance
Lightning Source LLC
Chambersburg PA
CBHW060701030426
42337CB00017B/2714